Garden*house*

Garden*house*

BRINGING THE OUTDOORS IN

PRODUCED BY BONNIE TRUST DAHAN
TEXT BY VICTORIA WISE
PHOTOGRAPHS BY SEAN SULLIVAN
STYLING BY ANTHONY ALBERTUS

CHRONICLE BOOKS
SAN FRANCISCO

Library of Congress
Cataloging-in-Publication Data available.

ISBN 0-8118-1910-8

Printed in Hong Kong.

Text by Victoria Wise
Photographs by Sean Sullivan
Styling by Anthony Albertus
Designed by Sandra McHenry Design

Distributed in Canada
by Raincoast Books
8680 Cambie Street
Vancouver,
British Columbia V6P 6M9

10 9 8 7 6 5 4 3

Chronicle Books
85 Second Street
San Francisco,
California 94105

WWW.CHRONICLEBOOKS.COM

It would have been impossible to
complete this project were it not for
the kindness and generosity of so many
people who let us into their homes.
Thank you all very much.

The Bates Family
The Boonville Hotel
Sharon Campbell
Michael Connell and Sandra McHenry
Allan Davis
Dom Dimento and Craig Lyall
Jeffrey Doney
Jim Dorsey
Pamela Fritz
Celia and Scott Graeber
Tomi Kushner
Ian Nabashima and Henry Kahle
Jean Neblett
Gerald Reis
Sally and Don Schmitt
Elena Silva
Jonathan Staub
Janice Stitt
Wendy and Fred Testu
Karen Thompson

Acknowledgments:

One of the pleasures of creating *Garden House* has been my
intimate association with the team of individuals whose talent,
dedication, and generosity of spirit transformed this enterprise
into a collective vision that we shared with exuberance and joy.
Their passion for perfection and deep affection for the garden
never failed to inspire my own efforts. If the theme of this book
is about bringing the garden indoors, both literally and figura-
tively, in a parallel way I feel fortunate to have brought their
ideas into this book to grace its pages, and I am deeply
indebted to:

Editor Leslie Jonath, who had the prescience to toss out
the first seed that germinated into *Garden House* and helped me
nurture it to full bloom.

Victoria Wise, for finding words to complement and
enhance the images and capture the essence of garden
house living.

Sean Sullivan, for his imagination, sensitivity, and photo-
graphic artistry that transformed what was in my head into
inspiring images.

Anthony Albertus, whose impeccable sense of garden style
and keen eye for detail is evident on every page of this book.

Sandy McHenry, for her elegant design sensibility that wove
the words and pictures together into a cohesive whole.

All the gracious and hospitable people who invited us
inside and shared the inventive ways to create a garden house.

I also must express my heartfelt gratitude to the hundreds
of gardeners in many parts of the world who profoundly affected
my personal connection to the garden. Their resourceful and
often whimsical interpretations expanded my ability to see all
aspects of what a garden can be and gave me permission to
bring it indoors.

—Bonnie Trust Dahan

Contents

Introduction

Once there was a garden called Eden. It was a joyous place, so benign and accommodating there were no boundaries between house and garden. Its one undivided space provided food, safety, and beauty for all its inhabitants. It was paradise. ❧ That story is ancient and perhaps never literally true, yet the myth of Eden remains a leitmotif of our dreams and wishes, a supreme metaphor for heaven on earth. ❧ In photographs and words this book reinterprets the setting of the myth, the unified place for our modern lives. Having been expelled from paradise, in an atavistic impulse to return we regain a bit of Eden by creating a garden house. ❧ A garden house is your indoor world as an extension of the natural world, not cut off from the realms of soil, sun, and growing plants. Making such a place relies more on having a gardener's aesthetic in the approach to interior design and decoration than on having a large space or a large budget. It does not depend on extensive remodeling or expensive materials. Rather, it takes a state of mind that doesn't hesitate to blur the ordinary distinctions between outside and in, that gathers them together into one artful unit in an interior that weaves an array of objects and outdoor life into a living tapestry. ❧ The textures, colors, and forms furnish and decorate the house; indeed the very scents that extend throughout take their cue from garden materials and artifacts. The ceiling or walls, in an inspirational play that brings the outside in, may be crosshatched with handcut twigs or with

An assemblage of canterra stone pots, a carved wooden pineapple, and a moss-filled garden urn welcome visitors to the garden house.

White tulips, stems submerged in a well-worn watering pitcher, create a visual haiku of the gardener's aesthetic and show how it neatly couples tender spring growth with the ancient things of the world.

weathered wood fencing. Clerestories open to the sky, and windows and doors reveal the outdoors. Mirrors may be used to widen narrow interiors and to reflect natural light, opening the space further to the outdoors. A bathing spot outside, but still accessible to the comforts of the house, incorporates the garden as an auxiliary room that amplifies the interior in an especially garden house way. ❦ Furnishings — seats, tables, beds, counters and desks to work upon, for both comfort and daily exigencies — can also give an aura of the garden. Intent on being **with** the garden even when not in it, the garden lover may bend rules in surprising ways: a park bench in the dining room, a hammock hung in a sunny spot in the house, a work desk amidst the flats of germinating plants in a greenhouse. ❦ The improvisations can go on and on, not only with furniture but with decorative accessory elements, too. Bottles of oil and vinegar, each differently flavored with sprigs of floating herbs; a miniature watering can set on the desk to hold pencils and pens; a kitchen counter filled with bouquets of flowers and vegetables that crowd out the chopping space — all provide connections to the garden and render the ordinary extraordinary. ❦ The spirit of the garden house is most manifest in its recognition that any outing, whether into one's own garden or beyond, can provide potential for interior decoration. If you have a yard, whether you have the time and patience for the work of gardening or prefer a natural disarray, just meandering in it can lead you to something to pick, pluck, or prune and carry in. Rather than frown at the rose bushes no longer blooming and in need of pruning at season's end, the garden house gardener exclaims at the unending loveliness of nature. The hips can be snipped off, brought inside, and arranged with some crabapples, their seasonal compatriot. Rosaceae both — the one grown for its flowers, the other for its fruit — rose hips and crabapples together form a picture of profound beauty, displaying both the diversity and eternally reconnecting paths of natural things. ❦ A stroll in the park can produce the same results. A twig found with a butterfly chrysalis attached, a broken-off branch of a flowering tree, a child's ball left over from the summer become treasures when viewed with the gardener's eye. The chrysalis is placed in a jar, covered with gauze, and set aside so it can complete its metamorphosis to butterfly or moth and be released to the garden again. The stem is set in a vase in the entryway where it greets all who enter as it develops into blossom. The ball is scooped up with some of its leaf nest and placed in a basket to grace the hearth and to remind one of summer in the light of winter fires. All — twig, stem, leaf, branch — provide opportunities

Iceland poppies are one of the most forgiving spring-to-fall blooming perennials. Suitable for both temperate and cold climates, they grow firm and tall without frost, yet will withstand it. Long lasting in a vase, they stand high on their stems and provide color and grace in any corner of the house.

for both decoration and stories when they are examined and appreciated with the garden lover's eye. ❋ To exemplify the gardener's aesthetic at play in our lives, this book is organized by the activities we engage in throughout the day and week. Whatever the abode — be it a twenty-room mansion with acres of grounds or a walk-up studio — bathing, working, relaxing, preparing food, dining, and sleeping pretty much define our mundane existence. The photographs in this book show artful and creative ways that anyone can adopt or adapt to bring those realms of the house and the garden together again. They show how the garden lover rethinks greenery, artifacts, and icons of the garden, however humble or grand, as elements of interior design and, in doing so, creates a garden house that recaptures a bit of Eden. ❋ The creators of this book hope its views open new horizons for you and inspire you to create a garden house of your own.

Around the world the pineapple motif is used in both interior and exterior decorating. Displayed anywhere from lamps to wrought iron gates, it symbolizes hospitality and refreshment. At thresholds it bids welcome to all who enter.

R e l a x i n g

One of the glories of the garden is the simple peace and respite found there. In our busy lives relaxing has become an anomaly, if not taboo. The garden house offers a domain of natural tranquillity; the splendor of the garden and its artifacts remind us that it's important to take time out. Around and about the corners, in and out of the views, vignettes and icons of the outdoors help in both ethereal and solid ways to regain the art of relaxing. ❧ The house's entrance captures the feel of a bower marking the beginning of the path through

A hefty white birch log with short spires of young branches is stood upright in the entryway and reinvented as a hall tree. It speaks of home, a place to hang your hat and relax.

a garden. An arrangement of nature's souvenirs collected during a quiet walk in the woods greets the homecomer and the day's cares can be shrugged aside with a deep sigh. In a stem vase in a hallway niche the last rose before winter imparts its scent, its singular charm a reminder that there's pleasure to be taken in small gestures. The sight of the emerging leaves and tendrilling roots of narcissus bulbs, established indoors in time to bloom before the winter holidays, can bring a springtime energy to weary steps. A bouquet of tulips set in front of an empty picture frame on the mantel elicits a smile that may deflect the day's worries: the bed's not made; the floor needs sweeping; the shelves need dusting; the groceries need to be gotten; but these sometimes-too-dominating tasks can be temporarily set aside to indulge in a moment's relaxation. ❧ The garden house encourages such fleeting visions and sensations, which open a quiet space in the mind that grants rest.

Relaxing is, after all, a quiet activity, the art and skill of putting oneself into an unrushed, softly breathing but still conscious frame of mind. Necessity and urgency are momentarily cast aside, restoring energy for further business. ✻ A spot in which to sit in view of the garden or within its aura provides opportunities for extended relaxation. Furnishing the setting in innovative ways creates an outdoor feeling inside. The seating may be a patio bench, a lawn chaise, a porch swing, or a garden chair. Side tables, coat racks, and sconces may be fashioned of tree parts, with stumps for tables, lengths of cut logs for clothes racks, and carved wood burls for wall shelves. The very ceilings may be joisted with timbers hewn from logs and left uncovered to expose their reassuring strength. Surrounding plants may sit in pots on the floor, stand on garden pedestals, or be potted in garden urns. Cut flowers may be contained in a galvanized bucket and a wrought-iron plant étagère may display garden pottery or discreetly serve as a telephone table. Windows may be dressed with gauzy material that provides both privacy and filtered light, or they may be left bare except for a frame of almost sky-high branches. An awning may be hung vertically to mark off a private space for repose on an indoor porch. All such elements of design call upon garden images to encourage a mood of relaxation. ✻ These are the settings for practicing the art of relaxing in garden house style. When it's time to have a seat and take a break, there's a place to do so. In midmorning or at dusk you can sit a while and feel the breeze that wafts through the window or doors wash away your cares; let bird songs open your ears to gentle garden pleasures; admire the sun's shadowy painting on the wall as its light filters through the ficus. The goals and designs of harried daily existence shrink away as time is spent in praise of shadows and the peaceful attention that is the essence of relaxing.

A sheaf of rushes fanning out of a simple glass vase set on the side mantel above the fireplace brings together water and warmth, flexibility and firmness. It's a relaxing sight for all who gather there.

Grasses potted to contain their natural exuberance for overtaking the garden are set on the hearth to provide supple texture against the hard, sheltering wall. The juxtaposition creates a subtle and artful balance between the bending and the unbending.

Rebuilt with sensitivity to the earth and a keen eye to incorporating whatever materials and objects could be reclaimed from the property after a devastating fire, this house, as one architect described it, exhibits a true rebirth of the site. Here we see the fireplace and its surrounding wall and mantels of poured concrete framed with timbers cut from huge trees left lying after the fire. Rushes and grasses from the reborn garden add a living element and pay homage to the continuing reemergence of nature.

13

Garden Furniture Indoors

A garden house is a home that reflects the gardener within. And so garden furniture may well furnish the house, or at least parts of it. Interior garden furniture makes a design statement about the environment the garden lover wishes most to be in — the garden — and shows off the carefree way in which license is taken to bring the outdoors in. The initial impetus may be a matter of economics: simple patio furniture like a small metal sidewalk table and chairs can be quite inexpensive and yet fit the bill for immediate furniture needs.

Or it may be a chance inspiration out of necessity: Here, this rickety camp table will hold my extra books for the moment. The first step can also be a luxurious indulgence, a commissioned dining table crafted of the finest wood and stone or an antique wrought-iron chaise longue to serve as a sofa. Whether begun for love or for money, the payoff for such resourcefulness may surprise you and open new horizons of interior decorating: go ahead and install a porch swing indoors if it pleases you.

An Adirondack chair in the living room, cozy to the fireplace, backlit by the sun coming in through the tall windows that open onto the garden, invites a restful pause. It's a gardener's indoor spot to perch, just for a moment, as you would in the garden. Not so cushy that you would sink in and forget your chores, it's comfortable enough for you to relax and admire the just-trimmed myrtle topiary or the flowering almond branches in a watering can that is placed in the sun's rays.

An empty picture frame and a bucket of books can lead to relaxation in garden house style. The frame is placed on the mantel to await its picture. The bucket is set on the floor beside a chair. For now, a bouquet of tulips fills the frame three-dimensionally. The books are at your fingertips ready for you to read, maybe after a brief catnap.

For the avid gardener who prunes and snips for relaxation, a bonsai-size topiary can satisfy that impulse indoors even when there's no outdoor space for the giant topiaries so famous in grand English gardens. A miniature topiary frame, this one in the shape of a carrot, accents this process by which plant becomes sculpture.

A telephone answering corner is furnished with a rocking chair and a plant étagère. Sunny garden colors, bamboo green for the chair and daffodil yellow for the plant pots, whisper of the garden and the respite it affords. The phone is discreetly placed at the very bottom of the étagère. Altogether, it seems a place for quiet conversation and simple relaxation.

17

In an ingenious use of natural elements the ceiling beams in this southwestern-style living room are inset with hand-cut red willow twigs gathered in New Mexico. More red willow twigs in a pottery urn, a freestanding bundle of them on the hearth beside it, and on the side table branches of arbutus with berries intact all display the owners' love of warm, dry climates.

Earthy tones and textures continue the theme of warm relaxation. A Mexican terra-cotta tree of life in the mantel niche, the sisal carpet on the floor, and a young olive tree in the corner further allude to the landscapes of drought tolerant gardens and rocky hillsides.

Like an old-fashioned mudroom designed to bridge the transition from the out-of-doors into the house, the entryway to this country house melds the inside and outdoors in a casual way. It's a place to remove your hat and coat, and to sit and take off your muddy shoes. A twig porch chair, a pile of those muddy shoes imprecisely stacked on the floor behind it, and the coat rack in full view, all indicate an unfussy approach to coming home to relax.

The wooden hall hutch on the other side of the entrance, laden with memorabilia of the out-of-doors, bespeaks a love of the country. A small vase of hydrangeas and an orchid in full bloom show the owner's love of the tended garden as well as the natural landscape. The horticultural lithographs propped on the floor against the wall and the unfilled garden-pottery amphoras in either corner tell us the sights and textures of the garden are more important to this garden house owner than either frippery or formal interior decorating.

21

Gardeners love roses because they're pretty, fragrant, and almost indestructible, surviving through frost and heat. Even if not always in their best state of show, they're prolific, offering up abundant flowers that move happily from bush to vase. In a mad passion for roses, this garden house features chairs covered in a rose-pattern fabric set on a rose-pattern rug. The French doors open onto the patio that sports a wicker settee cushioned with rose-motif pillows, with a rose garden visible behind it all. The child's rocker, hand painted in rosy colors, is placed close to a vase of roses so its occupant can enjoy their perfume.

A straw hat on the chair awaits your move to the garden. A planter of Erlicher narcissus on the breakfast table beckons you to join the outside.

Dreams of Paris, with its multitudinous parks, public gardens, urban greenways, and sidewalk cafes, have inspired these garden lovers to furnish their urban home with French outdoor furniture. The bistro table and chairs and a park bench provide the seating in the sun-stroked room that looks out onto a street scene beyond. It's a place to be at ease, to enjoy a morning coffee as the breeze billows the curtains through the open windows, and maybe to do a little background reading in a garden book before beginning the day.

A screened-in porch adjacent to the bedroom has been outfitted with a crude wooden garden chair, a tree stump side table, and lots of plants to create a gardener's respite spot. Protected from the elements, it's a nook that allows indoor relaxation in verdant surroundings, a haven where you can listen to the sound of the falling rain without getting drenched.

Cymbidium orchids in cast-stone planters set on either side of a reproduction antique-French rocking chair create an inviting and refreshing corner of repose. Like all green plants, the orchids take in carbon dioxide during the day and emit oxygen at night, and thus are natural air purifiers. The sun filtering through the floor-to-ceiling windows acts as a natural solar heater.

27

Capitalizing on the high-ceilinged, airy, light-filled space, this garden house living room is designed in unabashed praise of the outdoors. To accent the open space, two tall birch tree branches, here in their deciduous state, serve as window dressing. Antique French garden furniture furnishes the room. Old-fashioned plants — verbascum, trailing ivy, ficus, branches of green galax leaves — garnish the tables and embellish the corners. Complete with antique tricycle, the scene evokes an old European town park where adults gather to gossip, discuss, and munch while the children play about. It's an interior that presents an image of out-door community-style relaxation.

The walls, ceiling, and seats are appointed with artifacts the artisan owners and friends have crafted themselves, such as the crewelwork pillows stitched with a leaf motif. An extravagant impastoed picture frame with its mosaic of stained-glass flower petals attracts the eye as much for the beauty of the frame as for the small photo within.

Objects in the Room

Utilitarian and outdoor objects reinvented and re-arranged inside are a hallmark of the resourcefulness and creativity seen in this garden house. If one day, weeding out a neglected back bed of the garden, you run across some old medicine bottles, you may wonder how they landed there. The spontaneous reply is: It doesn't matter, today they would make lovely vases for tiny cuttings.

Rousting about in the back of the garden may turn up a rusty soil sieve; it would be perfect for that small wall you've been thinking of embellishing. Polished up, it's no longer a riddle; it's a decoration. A burly hunk of wood, perhaps an architectural relic once used as a corner brace, resonates with newfound light. Rein-vented as a wall sconce, it can hold a small, trailing plant that needs light and elevation to prosper. A glass cloche, originally intended to cover seedlings and facilitate their germination when the weather is not yet warm enough, is placed over a papier-mâché heart. The composition satisfies the garden lover who, beholding it, might muse: Yes, a museum-worthy piece, and all for the fun of it.

On the mantel a plethora of rosebuds that are too late to achieve full bloom have been collected and arranged in a four-square of small crates saved just because they're so appealing. Enclosed with mesh, the assemblage becomes an objet d'art that satisfies the gar-dener's artisan, thrift, and designer instincts all at once. The chandelier, looking almost like a candelabra, sends dappled light through leaf filigree and elegantly illumines the objects in the room.

An outdoor swing and an awning on an indoor porch solve the problem of where to sit in this small home. This is a private spot for bridging the sometimes conflicting intentions of resting inside and getting out to the garden. In it the gardener can swing softly, elbows supported by cushions, a blanket to throw on if it's chilly, while quietly regarding the implied tasks of those pruning shears, which will be taken up only after some stolen moments of respite.

C o o k i n g

The kitchen of the garden house is

heart and hearth of the home, the place where we seek to restore the connection between earth and table and ourselves. ❋ As the heart, the garden house kitchen is the nexus of the garden brought indoors. Whether from the property's acreage, from a small plot outside the kitchen door, or the farmers' market, the garden house kitchen is stocked with fresh garden gatherings. That may amount to a bushel of apples or a peck of olives for putting by or an armful of

A fork, propped tines down on a kitchen window ledge in the middle of a tomato row, is there not for a cutlery purpose but for the sheer beauty of its form.

fresh herbs cut and brought in to dry before the winter chills them into dormancy. It may be a basket of carrots or beets pulled from the kitchen garden, their leaves dew-dropped and roots still caked with dirt. They invite an earthy dish. More simply, twelve stalks of asparagus, six apricots, and one shallot selected from the spring market create a kitchen bouquet and inspire the cook to make up a dish for the new season. ❋ As the hearth, the garden house kitchen is where friends and family gather. They help prepare the meal and mill about discussing the day's events. Sometimes little cooking goes on around this modern hearth because often people have scant time or inclination to prepare meals from scratch. Yet, there is an abiding value to making the main meal of the day an important one. The very process of preparing food has the power to nurture and to restore, and people converge and assemble in the kitchen and dining room as much for good companionship as for the meal to

come. ❀ To accommodate this dual role of the kitchen as both heart and hearth of the home, the area is designed with company in mind. Minimally, it may be one wall of a small cottage with no pantry space to speak of and barely enough square footage for the cook to attend the stove. In a modest space nicely remodeled with a Corian counter and a built-in dishwasher, there may be sufficient room for a small garden bench or wooden stool by a window overlooking the garden, giving the cook respite or a guest a spot to sit. In a playful kitchen design the refrigerator may sport a facade of garden fencing and a funky metal garden chair can be nudged between the counter and refrigerator. In a lavish setting a kitchen poshly outfitted with sleek, bead-shaded overhead lights, marble counters galore, and a professional batterie de cuisine, leaves plenty of room to situate a comfortable wicker chair within range of the hearth. It's there for a browse through a new cookbook or for the cook's companion to sit and chat as the cooking is done. ❀ Whatever the scale and furnishings, the garden house kitchen brims with icons of the garden and the growing earth. Iron étagères display pots of edible and decorative flowers; garden trellises serve as racks for pots, pans, and kitchen towels; terra-cotta containers hold kitchen utensils; and baskets hold produce to be stored at room temperature. The kitchen calendar is a wire-bound sheaf of horticultural lithographs of seasonal produce that present new ideas for each month's cooking as the pages are turned throughout the year. A snippet or two of this and that make a miniature bouquet of fresh cuttings on the ledge over the sink. It is not a paltry offering, but as much a gift from the garden as the bushels and

A deep sink, installed for the varied purposes of washing fruit and vegetables as well as pots, for watering plants, and for arranging flowers, has become the hearth in this modern garden house in which family and friends collect in the kitchen to share camaraderie over food and gardening.

bunches of produce that make the meal. As the old children's tale expounds, even a stone soup, concocted of the lowliest provisions boiled up in a pot, can magically turn into a grand offering that brings happiness to the table if, from cabbage to onion to personal company, each adds a little and shares what there is to be had.

A potting bench, reinvented as indoor shelving, provides pantry space in the kitchen. There's room on the bottom to store a sack of potatoes, bowls of ripening fruit, and a wicker wine caddy. The middle tier holds baking ingredients and a rolling pin, right at hand for bread making. The narrow top shelves sport a collection of containers and antique biscuit tins filled with spices.

At olive harvest time the kitchen of this garden house becomes a hub of activity centered around the curing of olives. The process is a kind of culinary alchemy that turns the fruit, unpalatable in its natural state, into gems of the table. Here the olives, precured for many days to leech out the bitterness, are packed into jars and await the aromatic brine bath that will finish the curing and add flavor. Bundles of rosemary, bay, and garlic, hung to dry on the pot rack, have supplied some of their leaves to season the brine. A countertop topiaried olive tree and freshly picked lemons enhance the Mediterranean feel of the kitchen. The cook records notes about this season's recipe variations — maybe some lemon zest this time.

In a casual, suit-yourself way, this kitchen resonates with the garden and landscape around it and shows the lengths to which a garden lover may go in order to establish outdoor spirit in the house. The work table is a recycled yard bench. A section of fencing was recently installed on the wall, intended to be a pot rack, as soon as the hooks are attached. A rusty metal garden chair, set between the table and the refrigerator, is there to accommodate company and for a chat about how to prepare the winter squash on the table.

In flagrant disregard for convention the standard doors of the refrigerator have been cleverly facaded with custom-cut sections of fencing. Plants and bouquets embellish the room from top to bottom. Branches of fresh lemons are set high and out of the way in the ceiling fixture that's been emptied of lights and now playfully provides extra storage space. The top of the refrigerator, crowned with a ceramic pickling canister filled with drying yarrow and sage, lends additional shelf room. The freezer door holds a hanging planter filled with a bouquet of hydrangeas. It's a kitchen that shows the joy of the garden in all its natural and constructed variations, from plants to tools, wood to produce, artifacts to edibles.

41

The Timeless Kitchen

As everyday as cooking and eating are, the utensils
and ingredients of food preparation span the ages.
In a home kitchen that honors the beauty of old tools,
respect is maintained for their use in fixing and providing the modern meal. A wire lettuce-drying basket of
the sort you stepped outside to spin is filled here with
freshly picked persimmons. A tin food container that in
another era might have held some precious dried spice
is now used as a pot for growing a miniature plot of
wheat grass. A Florentine glazed-pottery bowl is filled
with floating flower petals freshly plucked as a subtle
reminder of the outdoor palette. Euphorbia stems in a
speckled blue pitcher reminiscent of the fifties will
move from kitchen to table when the meal is served.

In this timeless kitchen, a metal trough
originally meant to hold watered plant pots while they
drained now does the same service for the washed
dishes. Guava, grapefruit, pears, and onion form a
delectable display as they await their contribution to
the day's repast. A weighing bar mounted on the wall
is perfectly balanced between its twin vases. In an
amusing garden house twist, time itself is literally hung
up. A watch and its fob dangle from a hook, maybe still
telling time, maybe not. If so, it tracks time with a
muted ticktock that can be ignored if other projects
engage the mind.

On the counters of a vegetable gardener's kitchen, sprightly and colorful offerings have been assembled into an enticing edible array that seduces the eye, stimulates the mind, and sets the hands to cooking. Stalks of asparagus, newly emerged from their winter dormancy with still unfurled heads, have revealed themselves amidst their protective enclosure of ferny leaves and been cut for the table. They stand upright in a daffodil yellow vase that preserves their freshness until it's time to steam them. A bouncy assortment of red and yellow tomatoes in various sizes from cherry to medium are washed and draining in their mottled indigo blue colander. Together they create a picture all on their own. Delicate banners of lettuce leaves, not yet plucked, stand ready in their pot. A spray of homegrown lavender hung to dry on the wall lends purple tones and fragrance to the occasion. Hand-painted garden pots hold necessary kitchen utensils. All together, it's a room-filling potpourri, an ensemble doing a lilting dance between spring and summer, promising a salad that brings together some of the best of both seasons.

On the counters of a vegetable gardener's kitchen, sprightly and colorful offerings have been assembled into an enticing edible array that seduces the eye, stimulates the mind, and sets the hands to cooking. Stalks of asparagus, newly emerged from their winter dormancy with still unfurled heads, have revealed themselves amidst their protective enclosure of ferny leaves and been cut for the table. They stand upright in a daffodil yellow vase that preserves their freshness until it's time to steam them. A bouncy assortment of red and yellow tomatoes in various sizes from cherry to medium are washed and draining in their mottled indigo blue colander. Together they create a picture all on their own. Delicate banners of lettuce leaves, not yet plucked, stand ready in their pot. A spray of homegrown lavender hung to dry on the wall lends purple tones and fragrance to the occasion. Hand-painted garden pots hold necessary kitchen utensils. All together, it's a room-filling potpourri, an ensemble doing a lilting dance between spring and summer, promising a salad that brings together some of the best of both seasons.

Aloe All Around

Every garden house should have an aloe vera plant. Though it's not often praised for its beauty, it has fine form, and its medicinal power to soothe itching and heal minor burns is well documented.

It's an accommodating plant, too. In mild climates, you can grow aloe outside in sunny, not-too-wet corners of the garden or deck. In hot summer and chilly winter climates, aloe fares best as a potted plant that you bring indoors in the fall and return to the garden in late spring. Or, you can grow it as an indoor plant in a filtered-light spot where the sun warms the room but doesn't bake it. Indoors is the most convenient way to have aloe readily available for medicinal purposes.

To use aloe as a salve, cut off a piece of one of the thickest outside leaves. Pare away the thorny, prickly edges along the sides of each leaf so that you don't scratch yourself. Slice the section in half lengthwise to expose the gelatinous, viscous juices.

To treat insect bites, poison ivy or oak rashes, or minor sunburns, rub the juices over the traumatized area. Repeat as often as needed with fresh aloe juice until you feel relief from the sting or pain.

To treat other minor burns, place the trimmed and split-open aloe leaf directly on the injured spot, juicy side against the skin. Secure the leaf there with adhesive or gauze wrap and leave for at least six hours, or overnight. Repeat the process with fresh aloe and a fresh wrap for one or two days, until the pain is relieved and you no longer have any blistering around the burn.

47

The kitchen of this apple farm is a working space par excellence, well appointed with wood cabinets, butcher block countertops, a commercial stove top with a wide oven, and two extra-deep copper sinks. The apples, both heirloom and modern varieties, inundate the premises at harvest time; the kitchen layout is arranged to accommodate their bounty along with other kitchen-garden produce.

Whether they will be juiced, sliced, sauced, or eaten out of hand, apples need a brief washing first. The large center island is approachable all around, with a good expanse of counter space on two sides — the better to make room for many hands at its work top. Its deep and wide sink and modern water spout, tall and high, allow room for the big buckets and colanders that get turned around in the sink well as large batches of fruit are washed and drained. When it's time to have something besides apples, there's a loaf of freshly baked bread to slice.

49

D i n i n g

Meal time in the garden house is more than

eating — it's dining. Whether the fare is take-out, order-in, slapdash, or gourmet, the romance of the meal is as consequential as the food served. Whatever the space and its accommodations, the romance is created by an environment that takes its ambient cues from the garden, with a table set to include reminders of the season. ❧ The dining area may be a corner of the kitchen with barely enough room to fit a small table for two. It may be a somewhat larger dining nook that seats four in comfort. Or it may be a spacious dining hall intended for entertaining numerous guests. ❧ Walls can be decorated with old wooden fencing, a pleasing fancy that stimulates recollections of field trips in search of wildflower meadows and picnic spots. Shelves and side tables ornamented with miniature topiaries, potted ivy, and wheat grass will call up other outdoor associations. Garden hand tools, rethought and embraced as significant cultural artifacts rather than mere work implements, may be displayed for their fundamental beauty. The table may be a rough-hewn shed door turned horizontally to serve as a dining surface; a metal bistro table, a little rusty but still serviceable; or a finely crafted wooden groaning board. ❧ Cramped or copious, rustic or elegant as the situation may be, the table is set to suit the occasion and the season. In autumn or winter or after nightfall, candles are lit to illumine the table, their glow wrapping a kind warmth around

A side table set with traditional white crockery, a pitcher of alchemilla, and a vase of roses beckons guests to the dining room.

A green ceramic cabbage-leaf bowl on the table cheerily hints there's soup to start. Atop an earth-brown glazed dinner plate, the setting suggests it may be garden soup.

the meal. In spring or summer, when light fills the day for more hours, a freshly filled candelabra on the table or sideboard may be there mostly for effect. The pristine white wicks will be lit if necessary; otherwise, it's for show. ✹ Fruits and vegetables — lemons in spring, tomatoes or flowering herbs in summer, parsnips or rutabaga in winter — exhibit the bounty gathered from the garden or from the farmers' market. In the dark of winter, diminutive garden urns filled with moss, herbs bundled to dry in empty flagons, and clove-spiked oranges waiting to be hung on the holiday tree serve as decorative centerpieces that continue the theme of garden house dining year round. ✹ In a flight of fancy the napkins are folded origami style to resemble birds and are perched aside each plate. Radishes cut and soaked to open like roses, or oranges sliced and twisted into intriguing loops sit like shining jewels on each plate. In wily, tongue-in-cheek garden house style, the garden lover may employ benign artifice and toast garlic or cinnamon sticks and cloves, more to scent the house with their welcoming smell than to include in a dish. A flame orange-red ristra hung on the dining room wall is there for its gorgeous color, ceremonial significance, and artful form, although the host may not be particularly fond of eating chilies. Such whimsies make for good conversation regardless of the victuals or the expertise of the cook. ✹ All in all, the garden house host creates a dining scene with a spirit that moves freely between indoors and out. Striking an appropriate note for the hour and the season, the table and its environs, from lighting to room decorations, from table adornments to plate garnishes, are set to invite the heart's ease that comes from a tenderly tended meal in accord with the season.

Old garden tools — trowels, spades, a soil claw-cultivator — retired from outdoor service and recycled as decorations are displayed on a shelf above a window lintel. With the addition of laurel leaf wreaths and a garden motif pitcher, the grouping declares this to be a garden lover's dining nook.

In the gardener's aesthetic any container can be a vase and a vase can be filled with any cutting. Here we see fanciful interpretations of the gardener's approach to vases and their fill. The side stage is set with a trio of variously shaped glass containers, each with a different garden offering. One holds a narcissus bulb, another a euphorbia stem, and the third a Japanese maple branch. On the window-sill a begonia peeks out from a parade of potted narcissus. On the other side of the room empty sarsaparilla bottles serve as vases to hold more Japanese maple cuttings the gardener has brought in after the tree's annual pruning.

55

Moss on stone. In its quiet way it resonates with the almost total silence of a contemplative walk through a foggy landscape or footsteps on pristine ground. Its bright and fragile greenness, revealed on the rocks in the garden, in the cracks of the sidewalk, between the wood slats on the deck, or over the surface of plant pots, summons you to bend down, look closely, and take pleasure in the beauty of the moment. Gathered up in clumps and set in garden stoneware to decorate the table, the pots of moss, surrounded by candles, invite you to enjoy the flickering light of winter and discuss ancient things.

Setting the Seasonal Table

From glimmer to greenery, the table setting in a garden house is laid with special attention to lighting and table accessories that recreate the mood of the day or the season in the garden. When extra illumination is needed in the soft light of early spring or the dim light of mid-winter, it might be provided by miniature kerosene prism lanterns, a grouping of multilevel tapers or bees-wax candles, or a table candelabra of votives. When the sun sends its rays and solar warmth through the windows, and extra illuminaria are not required to see by, the candles may remain just for their own beauty and their promise of light. In summer a lush bough of grape leaves may be grandly spread along the center of the table. More modestly, a ribboned nosegay of lavender sprigs holding name cards may be delicately set on each plate. Two apples, one shiny red pomegranate, or a bottle of special olive oil may serve as a simple centerpiece.

In the autumnal setting at left, the table is decorated with fall colors and seasonal offerings. Crab-apples and rose hips arranged on a tiered candy server provide the centerpiece. Bouquets of fresh herbs perfume the table. A crackling fire in the background provides warmth, extra light, and a comforting sound that sings of autumn and the falling light.

In its unaffected elegance, this setting portrays a gentleman farmer's way of life, which includes land on which to grow things and an inviting dining room in which to gather friends and family to enjoy the provender. The room is sparsely decorated with earth tones and outdoor icons. The single wall ornament, a fragment of building art, provides an architectural dimension against the flat, ochre-colored walls. Two olive trees brought in for the occasion frame the doors to the garden and accentuate the focus of the scene: it's an autumn meal. In homage to the cultivated land upon which we all ultimately rely, harvest gleanings serve as centerpieces and signify the end of the growing season for this year.

A small room off the garden can provide
an informal dining nook that sings with
the spirit of the garden and grants direct
access to it. Here an indoor porch turns
into a dining room cum potting shed
that allows for chummy dining with the
garden. The chairs are springy and bouncy,
comfortable to sit on and easy to get
up from when the garden calls you to
change the water or to finish the bulb
planting after a bite to eat. A length of
fencing provides jerry-rigged — crude
but pleasing — wainscoting on the wall
behind the table.

The overhead shelf holds a set of hand-painted galvanized sap buckets filled with drying lotus pods that, on a quick glance, give the illusion of modernistic light fixtures. A large watering can just inside the window can be both a reminder of work well done and of more work yet to come. A rosemary topiary set in a biscuit tin speaks to the good care plants get here. All in all, inside and out are integrated in a dining spot both restful and lively.

63

A bird cage, with an enameled tin pitcher
full of euphorbia and date palm stems
perched on a stool in front of it, and
a section of fencing, cavalierly propped
against the wall, flank the pine plank
door. Now the old door, scrubbed and
rubbed, serves as a dining table. Long and
narrow, its dimensions are just right for
conversational intimacy across the table
as well as for plenty of guests down its
length. Its heft rests solidly on the frame
of a recycled garden workbench to provide an elbows-on-the-table sturdiness
for the repast.

Cabbage and many of its brassica kin come in colors and forms that are decorative as well as edible. There's no reason to keep the cabbage in the kitchen. An ornamental kale with its frilly upright leaves contrasts well with a pot of softer, fuzzy-leafed verbascum, or mullein. On the étagère in the corner of the dining room they provide greenery to embellish the room without taking up table space. When the dates in the other corner are so ripe they almost fall off their stems, they'll be plucked and used in the kitchen.

Along with the more predictable ornamental value of plants and flowers, in the
gardener's aesthetic any outdoor artifact
or garden motif is fair game to bring
inside and decorate the house. In this
dining room, the first thing that catches
the eye is a wrought-iron plant holder
hung at a jaunty angle. Free of the
weight of pots, it appears to be doing
a wheelie over the wood-shelf fixture
below it, where the plants are safely set.
A broadleaf ivy spills out of its ceramic
pot, which is mounted like a wall sconce.
A sunflower has been dried and displayed
in a picture frame. A dish of sprouted
wheat grass is displayed for its verdant
freshness, to be admired before it
is pureed into a healthful juice.

A hand-formed pottery dish is filled with a dozen araucana hens' eggs. Naturally colored in delicate hues from pale green to pastel blue and mottled brown, they're beautiful on their own, and they also hint of a good meal to be had. A lawn chair, with its seat and back of interwoven wide strips of die-cut metal reminiscent of the fifties and backyard barbecues, has been brought in to provide side seating in the dining room, or perhaps an extra place at table. A bowl of just-cut garden lemons, stems and leaves intact and in different stages of ripeness, is set on the table to provide bright color against the weathered wood table top. Altogether, the assemblage creates an aura of caprice and reveals a joy in eating, from garden to table to kitchen and back to the table again.

The garden calls out loud and clear in this modest dining spot in a small kitchen. A bouquet of nicely arranged poppies bedecks a plant étagère that also serves as a plate rack. The table is taken up with a pitcher of cut dahlias and zinnias plunked into a vase to keep them watered while they await further thoughts from the gardener. It must be early summer. The counters are spread with a row of potted flowers seemingly permanently ensconced there. The flat of pansies and violas on the floor wait their turn. Presumably the table will be cleared for lunch or dinner, but for now, there's a mug of tea to sip as the gardener plots further planting.

W o r k i n g

Whether you labor for love or for money, if you work in a garden house all aspects of work are integrated in an environment that permits both concentration and enjoyment of the process. That means, whatever the work, the surroundings must include a bit of the outside and allow for some dreaming, relaxing, and leisure, too. Garden house work spaces are places where one can practice the art of working, where the humdrum can be transcended and stress alleviated in a milieu that invites engagement in work in the best sense

A tiny portable clock discreetly reflects its image off the mirror-smooth desktop. Together they serve as a gentle reminder that there's a schedule to keep to, even in this otherwise timeless, dreamy, garden-imbued work space.

of the idea: complete and joyful participation in what one is doing, whether it be routine or challenging. ❧ In typical turn-about-is-good-play style, the garden lover imaginatively establishes a work space anywhere that lends itself to incorporating garden spirit. Why not furbish an open back porch with a writing desk, turn an airy dining room into a conference room, or set a work table in the center of a light-filled orangery amidst the citrus nurslings? The middle of the kitchen with view onto the garden; a breezy loggia with natural lighting to suffice in lieu of electrical fixtures; a commodious foyer with plenty of room for garden artifacts; a dirt-floored greenhouse — any might accommodate the job at hand. ❧ The desk or work top can be makeshift. It may be magnificently so, with a pair of cast-iron planter urns set in concrete column plinths to stabilize and elevate a slab of marble high enough to allow ample knee room underneath. A jerry-rigged wood plank set on sawhorses

more modestly, but facilely, serves the same purpose. In other venues a rough, unfinished bench on which to splay out seeds that need sorting doubles as a writing table for the gardener, and an extravagant antique secretary desk large enough to fill the center of a lofty room does the same. ❋ The actual work to be done may involve pen and paper, kitchen utensils, workshop tools, or a computer, telephone, or fax machine. Whether you endeavor to write the latest thoughts for an exegesis on gardens, surf the net for information on money investments, or network for the next theater job, garden elements are featured prominently in the garden house work space. ❋ The tools of the garden, especially when employed in unusual ways, can reconnect us with the earth as we ensconce ourselves in mind work. Pruning shears hung on the wall by the door dangle in front of a leaf-patterned background and serve as a decorative element while, at the same time, they are ready at hand for their original purpose. Farther from their original use but artfully, a trowel

An antique mud scraper fancifully rein-vented as a fruit bowl holds apples in its reservoir. Pen and notebook have been momentarily set aside so the worker can admire the shimmering light across the display.

becomes a paper clip holder; a gardener's tool bag becomes a fine brief case; and a miniature topiary form serves as a paper weight as long as the wind is not too strong. A harvesting basket is an obvious container for recyclable waste paper. ❋ In other large and small ways, the gardener stays attuned to the spirit of the outdoors while at work by embellishing the work space with icons and artifacts of the garden. A bark chip, lovingly picked up and brought home from a spur-of-the-moment children's game of Frisbee is displayed on the desk for no other purpose than as a reminder of that innocent joy. A cherub, once seated atop a stone column in the garden, now has a position of honor indoors on the mantel beside the desk. A bundle of citrus blossom prunings imparts an indescribable, delicious fragrance to the room. ❋ All these objects, sights, scents, and treasures of the garden lend a presence that abets concentration and infuses daily tasks with an uplifting spirit.

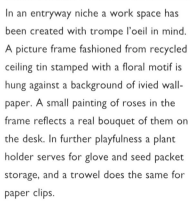

In an entryway niche a work space has been created with trompe l'oeil in mind. A picture frame fashioned from recycled ceiling tin stamped with a floral motif is hung against a background of ivied wallpaper. A small painting of roses in the frame reflects a real bouquet of them on the desk. In further playfulness a plant holder serves for glove and seed packet storage, and a trowel does the same for paper clips.

73

The overwhelming desire to be outdoors
in the warmth of the summer garden
when there's inside work to be done
has inspired this garden lover to devise
a work space on the front porch. Chair
and table are enclosed with a ceiling-to-
floor canopy of mosquito netting that
both staves off pesky insects and creates
a cozy cocoon within which to write
a book on pressing flowers.

74

In this indoor work space, a small desk with a marble top set on a verdigris wood base is nestled into a windowed corner with front and side views onto the garden. Delphiniums, sweet peas, and ceramic tiles painted with outdoor scenes populate the area. The table surface is crowded with garden books and long spouted watering cans, a small one to hold pens and a large one presumably to carry water. It must be that the garden paraphernalia and the outside views the space enjoys are more important than the square footage the table top allows for desk work.

In an attached greenhouse that has become both an indoor and outdoor work space, the greenery and its many accoutrements — pots, seedling flats, garden tools — have supplanted all else. It's a private and gleeful place where potting, germinating, and growing take precedence over any office work. So oriented to the garden is this gardener that the window is never quite closed because that would disturb the rose cane that has wended its way in from the outside, tucking its delicate, graceful spire of new growth into a place of honor in the work room.

Along the wood-slat countertop that allows for drainage when the plants are watered, a space has been cleared for the gardener's work. The terra-cotta containers of pens, pencils, and wood garden markers suggest that much of the normal work done here is writing down and identifying plants. For the moment, it's a place to write a note to a friend that says how hearty the coleus looks, unwithered by the recent cold spell, how well the scented geraniums are coming along, and offers to share some of last season's squash seeds, stored in bottles until the next planting season.

Rolled up blueprints stand upright in a large terra-cotta jug originally intended to hold olive oil. A wood ladder serves as a magazine rack for horticultural publications, and miniature topiary forms add sculptural elements to the drafting table desk. The greenhouse atmosphere of the sunny and well-lit space also allows the room to double as an orangery, a nursery to protect the potted citrus tenderlings from frost damage to which they are susceptible in cold weather. Under their aegis, the gardener maps out a blueprint for a landscape design that will feature the citrus when planted outdoors.

A dining room furnished with a teak garden table and chairs, a fern-motif rug, and a large potted palm is a space that permits serious conferencing as well as garden house–style dining. The chairs are cushioned and roomy enough for sitting back and pondering, but firm enough for sitting up and attending to the project at hand. The gentle tea green color of the walls helps to induce an atmosphere of calm for brainstorming. A bamboo garden rake transformed into a coat rack helps keep the proceedings somewhat light-hearted, the better to think by.

A dining room furnished with a teak garden table and chairs, a fern-motif rug, and a large potted palm is a space that permits serious conferencing as well as garden house–style dining. The chairs are cushioned and roomy enough for sitting back and pondering, but firm enough for sitting up and attending to the project at hand. The gentle tea green color of the walls helps to induce an atmosphere of calm for brainstorming. A bamboo garden rake transformed into a coat rack helps keep the proceedings somewhat light-hearted, the better to think by.

The Gardener's Aesthetic
and the Surprises It Allows

On a southeast-facing loggia overlooking the water, this gardener has set up a work space with the feel of being in a forest of plants while also basking in the sun and taking in the fresh salt air. The scene is full of the kinds of surprises that exhibit the gardener's aesthetic. A loggia is outdoors, but not in the garden, so here the garden is brought to it. The space is small, but a large mirror serving as a facade along one wall helps to give the feel of largesse one gets from being in a country garden. A prodigious number of shade-loving plants — like narcissi and begonias — which prefer airy spaces and filtered light, are settled around and about, sufficiently sheltered to thrive in splendor.

The salt air wisping off the bay is far enough removed to be diluted and not deposit too much salinity on the plants, but close enough for one to lean out and take a whiff of its refreshing cleanness. Perhaps most surprising is that in the midst of such a supremely lavish setting, with its Greek columns, wrought-iron railing, and high bay view, all this luxury is balanced by an informal, almost quirky take on the furnishings, like the folding outdoor side chairs and the simple round table for the office desk. It's a working space that shows how the garden aesthetic, whether formal or fanciful, can lead to an environment vibrant with the outdoors and imbued with garden spirit.

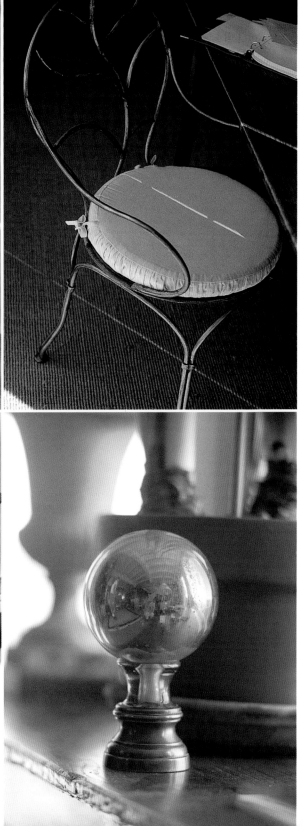

In an expansive space with a lofty ceiling, high arched windows, and walls painted a smoke-tinged lavender, a stylish secretary fills the center of the room. The desk itself is broad enough to accommodate a large amaryllis in glorious full bloom and two prepossessing lamps fashioned of iron urns, with plenty of work space left on its surface. Garden ornaments, a cast stone cherubim dangling a precious glass bauble, a finial from an outdoor lamp stand, and a bowl cushioned with a grass nest that beds stone eggs are set around the room as decorative fillips. They please the eye and mind of this garden lover, who has chosen a formal style of decorating that perfectly suits the grandiloquent interior.

85

B a t h i n g

Water, the essence of life, is celebrated in a garden house bathing place. In this chapter we see myriad ways the garden lover can design the bathing room to take advantage of water's cleansing and life-giving qualities. ❧ In a minuscule space with just enough room for a shower stall, a tiny window to crack open is highlighted with a wall-hanging mirror; together, they tease the eye to consider the outside and inside

Pots of long-blooming lace-cap hydrangeas happily reside in the humid warmth of the bathroom. When their soil needs moistening, the tub provides a natural and fitting watering place.

both. In an old-fashioned bathroom the tub, newly plumbed to accommodate a shower head, offers the choice of bath or shower, waterfall or pool. The light shining through the open window and bouncing off the brilliant white walls gives the feeling of being on a sunny hill in a Grecian village. ❧ In a more recently built bathing room, this tub of poured concrete brings to mind the sculptural possibilities for the bath and calls up memories of relaxing soaks in a rock-surrounded natural mineral bath. In another place the walls around the shower are made of rammed earth; solid and heartwarming at the same time, they signify the union of earth and water that provided the foundation for life on our planet. ❧ In two other locations avid garden lovers who consider the garden truly auxiliary to the house, not just outside it, have sidestepped convention and situated their bathing rooms in the garden. One, a shower, recalls perhaps the childhood joy of dancing in the rain, happily getting wet. The other, a tub, conjures an image of the respite to be found in a clear, quiet,

outdoor pool where there is nothing to disturb the peace except the minnows tickling your feet. ❈ In all these locations the garden lover takes cues from both natural and engineered sources of water to celebrate its restorative power and the contemplative solace to be found with it. ❈ As the bath is drawn or the shower is turned on, the room echoes with water's natural sounds, from the gentle babble of a running brook to the tinkle of raindrops on the roof to the roar of a cascading waterfall. As the steam rises the room glows with a warm mist that repeats the natural ecosystem where water-loving plants thrive. Orchids, ferns, and begonias decorate the room and create the illusion of showering in a miniature rain forest. Sprouts of seedlings that need moisture and heat to germinate luxuriate in the humid atmosphere while they grow sturdy enough to transfer to the soil. In handy proximity to the tub and sink, pots of water-loving hydrangeas and ivy flourish in the warm light. Cuttings of herbs and other aromatic plants placed on the counters or sills and around the water taps release their relaxing fragrance as the hot water flows. ❈ Other design details that usher in the garden and nature also reconnect bathing to its origin in the outdoors.

In a serene blending of indoors and out, floating gardenias and a garden bouquet temper the starkness of this poured concrete bathtub. A harvesting basket of fresh towels and a pair of bamboo slippers to step out of the tub into, lend extra plushness to the scene.

A vine trellis serves as a towel rack. Terra-cotta pots hold bayberry candles to light the room on dark days and perfume the air with a forest scent. Wood slat shutters that close to provide a screen for privacy during bathing can also be opened as the bather emerges to reveal the view onto the garden and to let the light in. Pictures of water fauna and fish, towels of combed cotton sweet to the touch and soft as newly grown moss, and bamboo slippers all complete a setting that invites you to revel in the water and the ritual of cleansing.

There's no need for fussy adornments
in this herb fancier's bathroom. The sun
streaming into the room decorates the
wall as it reflects off the bright white tiles
in circles of light and shadow and bathes
the simple, old-fashioned porcelain tub
in its glow. Catching the light on the window sill are canisters of herbs and bubble
bath gels promising scents and efferves-
cence in the bath. On the sink vanity, a
laurel-green glazed saucer holds the soap
and clear glass vases filled with aromatic
herbs offer up subtle scents.

Within a simple setting the herb fancier has designed a way to practice the art of bathing by creating a place to indulge in a veritable aromatherapy treatment right at home. As the bath is drawn the water runs through the sheaf of aromatic euca-lyptus and artemisia hanging over the tap and releases their soothing fragrances. As the steam rises from the warm water, it heats the room and activates the esters in the lavender, rosemary, and bay laurel cuttings filling the jars and canisters.

Pots of ivy are being watered in the basin as a cocoa-scented oncidium orchid on the counter tickles the mirror, and awaits its drink in the sink. A splendiferous bunch of freshly trimmed toyon branches awaits arrangement on a stool. The large sink and vanity, the focus of the scene, are formed of poured concrete. It's a water-friendly material that invites the bathing room to double as a watering shed for plants.

In the same room the walls, too, are
made of water-friendly material, this
time rammed earth. Sometimes called
pressed earth, it's similar to the adobe
bricks used to construct the floors, ceiling, and walls of Pueblo Indian houses.
Like adobe, rammed earth both allows
heat to escape and retains coolness, so
that, except in extremes of climate, a
pleasant living temperature is maintained
within the house. It also breathes and
dries, so water does not collect in its
nooks and crannies or pool on its floors
long enough to create algae and rust
buildup. And because it's earth, even
though pressed into solid-as-brick blocks,
there's a suppleness and resilience that
is not provided by porcelain, marble, or
other hard materials more typically used
to furnish and build the bathroom. The
sink and shower are both fitted with
nozzle handles more commonly seen
on outdoor plumbing fixtures. Such
design details accentuate the theme of
the outdoors brought in, the hallmark
of the garden house.

Tropical Adventures
Through the Orchid's Eye

So prolific is the Orchidaceae family that indigenous varieties are found on every continent except Antarctica. They grow with especial abandon in tropical regions everywhere, planting themselves in the loose, natural compost on the forest floor; attaching themselves to the middle of tree trunks to grow in the air; twining their way up any height as they exploit their ecological niches. The inexhaustible variety of their wild and wonderful forms and coloration elicits continual awe and has made orchids a favorite of gardeners everywhere. They are also a consummate house plant because their natural habitats are easily simulated indoors. In the absence of a solarium in which to grow, many varieties of orchids can be coaxed into bloom with a bit of light, a bit of shade, a bit of moisture, and a bit of warmth. True, a sturdy orchid vine such as the one that produces vanilla bean pods from its night-blooming flowers won't grow indoors, but oncidiums, paphiopedilums, cymbidiums, and dendrobiums, to name but a few of the genera, will. And the bathroom can be ideal for doubling as an orchid greenhouse. With its frequently misted and heated air, the moisture factor is taken care of without too much daily fussing. East or partially shaded west or south windows will supply the necessary filtered light, as will overhead skylights. Here a gargantuan pot of cymbidiums on the patio softens the light freely streaming through the clear-glass, west-facing window and protects the indoor growing plants from overheating. Inside, dendrobiums and more cymbidiums bloom tall and strong in their beautiful Asian pots. In and out of the window, this bath is an orchid adventure.

In this garden house bathing room, flamboyantly trimmed with plants in pitchers, small pots, and large garden urns, the tub seems to take second place. In a bow to the activity ostensibly intended for the room, a watering can holds some brushes and sponges for the actual bathing and scrubbing, but it's clear the keeper prefers to be outdoors, or at least to entertain garden dreams while relaxing in the bath.

97

Here, the garden house owner has taken full advantage of the wide doorway and background window to design the bathroom space in a playful replication of an early Renaissance decor. Standing in the hallway facing the room, prominent in the foreground we see the lime-green wall and creamy white doors that suggest an opening to a terrazzo. But rather than a terrazzo, what we step into is an interior delicately furnished with plants and garden fixtures that tease us to wonder whether we are inside or out. Approaching the sink, we can almost feel the gentle air rustling the filmy white curtains as our eyes are inexorably led to the narrow aperture revealing a view of the true outside.

Bathing Among the Plants

In a glorious rendition of the gardener's aesthetic, two garden house bathing spots depict how garden house richness is created as much with attitude and spirit as anything else. Incorporating the garden as an architectural element of the house, the bathing spots are situated directly in the out-of-doors, where the owners can, quite literally, bathe among the plants.

In one setting, an almost ancient porcelain tub, its cast-iron bottom exposed to full view, is plunked directly on the floor of the redwood deck, where water splashes cause no harm. It's an especially nice moment to bask in the bath and soak up the spectacle of lush spring growth and first-blooming flowers — freesias, primroses, azaleas — that frame the scene. The almost rococo, silver-finished mirror on the floor by the tub is positioned out of immediate sight so that the bather must lean out of the tub to gaze into it. It's a discretion that invites a muse to visit as the bather glides up to shoulder level in the warm bath.

In another setting an outdoor shower takes advantage of the privacy afforded in a small backyard enclosed by an undulating fence of pressed wood log rounds set at various heights to accommodate the land's contours. The uprights of the fence make a perfect hanging board for a back-scrubbing brush and leafy sponge. The cross brace serves as a shelf for the soap. Flowering maple, variegated canna, and a bucket of cut jonquils add a colorful trill to this outdoor symphony. One might imagine that, if showering at just the right moment, one could be privy to the native frogs breaking into their morning song, adding their own background staccato croak to the bathing serenade.

D r e a m i n g

Just

as a garden is a place to dream while one wanders along its paths, the garden lover, a quintessential dream weaver, knows that any interior can become a place for dreaming when the garden and its soothing grace are introduced into the room. ❧ An indoor garden room makes a paradisical bedroom. The garden may be invited into the house through wide open doors, and the imminence of its sights and scents caresses the owner's dreams. An indoor porch off a veranda, with light filtering in through a wall of screened windows and overhead skylights, is turned into a cozy day parlor and fair-weather sleeping room. A copious utility porch just inside the back door is reinvented as an afternoon rest spot with a pillowed hammock filling the room in place of laundry machines or pantry shelves. Although it takes a little effort to get into the hammock, once there, one does not hasten to get out. What could be better than to be lulled into the land of daydreams by its calming sway? A comfortable chaise in the corner of a sun-filled, airy drawing room can entice in the same way. A bit of daydreaming is irresistible as you nestle in. In a more cloistered setting, the interior bedroom of an urban house is set up as a green oasis that, with its lacy and verdant foliage, provides the peace and quiet of a private garden. ❧ In all of these venues, garden elements, artifacts, and icons set the stage for dreamy pleasures that echo the delights of being in the archetypical garden, the place where outside and inside were magically blended into

Books atop a garden stepladder within arm's reach of a sun-warmed hammock illustrate an inviting scene wherein a reader may swing gently into dreamland.

An old garden gate made of iron wrought in a spidery motif is mounted as a head-board on a meadow-green wall. The pillows, too, are embroidered with insect motifs. Friendly bugs are, after all, major players in any lively garden.

contented oneness. ✿ Whether it's a child's bed, a hammock for daydreaming, or an extravagant king-size expanse for spending an entire evening catching up on read-ing, the garden house takes into account that dreams, it seems, are pillowed. To induce sweet dreams, cushions, soft blankets, feather-filled comforters, and sheets and pillowcases of natural fiber dress the bed. When one is tucked into such places, eyelids can easily droop as a book slides unfinished into the covers. ✿ In more subtle ways, the garden house owner designs interiors made for dreaming. The walls are tinted in natural colors ranging from umber, sienna, and alabaster to garden greens — the hues providing a background canvas for three-dimensional decorations that continue the garden theme and encourage good dreams. The walls are adorned with anything and everything that whispers of the garden: wreaths woven from fallen twigs, and tree prunings intertwined with bird feathers and allium bulbs; flower and bush cuttings tied into potpourri bundles; framed lithographs and silkscreens of garden creatures from butterflies to hummingbirds, and of plants both edible and inedible. In a charming literal interpre-tation of the magical blending of outside and in, a child's wagon can hold both plants and a watering can filled and ready for the plants' morning refreshment. Baskets, hung on walls or placed around a room, also serve as containers for daily talismans as well as timeless matters. They may be filled with laundry or a collection of mending that really ought to be done, or better yet, with clean pajamas for tonight and fresh towels for after the bath in the morning. Or, as tokens of timelessness, they may remain empty, there to hold the impalpable dreams of today and promises for tomorrow. ✿ As the sun sets and shadows fade, under the aegis of such cushioned comfort and mind-pleasing visions, the garden house dweller floats into a contented slumber filled with aimless, blissful dreams.

Fragrance and foliage add sweet smells and peace to dreams. Here, in a second-story apartment bedroom without one-step access to the outdoors, a stupendous bouquet of snapdragons forms an umbrella over the bed and brings the garden upstairs. The simple lamp shade atop a carved-wood pineapple base is crowned with a bay laurel wreath. Perhaps its honor was earned, perhaps only dreamed of, but its fresh, rise-and-shine scent, exuded as the room warms each morning, arouses the sleepers before the clock has a chance to clang out its own, more jolting, wake-up call.

A wagon, red or yellow, rusty or shiny, was a way to carry hopes and dreams in childhood years. Here the traditional cargoes of rocks and toys have yielded to potted plants and a watering can. A garden-fence bedstead seems a good place to park the wagon at bedtime. The toy bear and shovels are in place on the chair, ready for tomorrow.

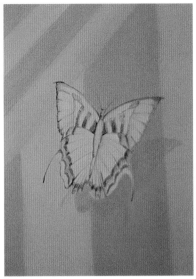

A bedroom that opens directly onto the garden may be a gardener's dream. The gardener can bed down with the outdoors without camping out, enjoying the peace of a garden along with the comforts of the house. On the walls and bedside tables within the room, pictures of birds, butterflies, and flowers supply fauna and flora. The French doors have been opened wide to the sensuality of the living garden with its plenitude of shrubs and overhanging foliage. The valise tucked well out of the way under the dressing bench suggests that traveling time may be over for now.

Baskets Empty and Full

Cardboard cartons are all right for basement storage: childhood art you can't bear to part with, miscellaneous electrical and plumbing connectors that might come in handy someday, and old tax forms that must be saved. But in the living space of the garden house, baskets serve as more elegant containers. Placed in the entryway, on the back porch, under the desk, beside the bath, or at the foot of the bed, they add their individual beauty to the environment. Empty, they suggest the mystery of what might be. Filled, they accomplish necessary organizing and containing of goods in a decorative way.

  Windows and doors opening onto the garden lend grace to daily living and bliss to nighttime dreaming. In a spacious setting a four-poster bed, each post finialed with a different suit of a deck of playing cards, has been positioned close to the scenic view directly outside and the doors have been swung open to bring it closer. A collection of Native American baskets in front of the bed hum a silent lullaby of ancient ways and indigenous art. As the day sets on the garden, the wrought-iron wall lamp provides a low, restful light and sheds its soft glow over the cozily covered bed. Topiaried santolina arranged on the bedside table season the setting with their pine scent. The easily mopped floor, fashioned of sealed terratile squares made from a mixture of earth and cement, permits going in and out without the fuss of removing shoes each time. Three cotton throw rugs strategically placed on the floor around the bed assure that bare feet will not be too chilled in the morning.

A spot for dreaming in this garden house features a reproduction Napoleonic chaise longue and a faux bois plant stand with legs in the form of tree roots underpinning a basket of blooming narcissus. The pairing creates a tableau of an old French courtyard in early spring.

As every kindergartner learns, *A* is for apple and the first letter of the alphabet, called alpha. *A* is also for alpha waves, the deep and restful state of sleep wherein we dream without threat of ghosts and hobgoblins. The wall is decorated with a wooden *A* collage adorned with a garland. The bedside stand is adorned with a triad of chartreuse, forties-era ceramic vessels: two filled with yellow-green proteus, the third left empty to be filled as the dreamer will. All together it's a setting that invites the sleeper to peaceful green dreams.

Originally an architectural staple of many houses, the screened-in porch was intended for summer use, often for sleeping. There was the added advantage that it was outdoors, not exactly in the open, able to catch any small gust of breeze, yet protected from the mosquitoes and other flying bugs in the sultry nights. New meaning has been given to the concept by designing a screened-in porch usable year round. During the winter, the screens are replaced with windows much like storm windows and the porch then doubles as a personal parlor in which to muse. In the spring, the windows are removed and the screens are set in place to allow fresh air circulation. To welcome daytime activities like working, and chatting as well, the bed retracts into a banquette. All through the year, the sun creates a kaleidoscope of patterns and colors that dance through the plants and reflect off the walls.

After stepping across the pine plank floor and settling into the bed with a potpourri purse on the fluffed-up pillows and turned-down duvet, the garden house traveler can gaze at the watchtower clock on the facing wall. It's comforting to know it won't ring in the morning. It was a good day out, and the breezy room filled with garden things might inspire a restful, stay-in-bed Sunday morning.

Resources

Without the incredibly wonderful people behind these stores, businesses, design studios, and nurseries, this book would never have been as easy to create. These are wholeheartedly endorsed resources.

Garden Antiques

Aria
1522 Grant Street
San Francisco, CA 94133
415.433.0219
Obscure antique garden and architectural ornament, lighting and furniture.

The Garden Trellis
8015 Maple Street
New Orleans, LA 70118
504.861.1953
Garden ornament, old and new, plants of a wild vein.

Interieur Perdue
340 Bryant Street
San Francisco, CA 94107
415.543.1616
Coco, Fred, and Fritzy's eclectic collection of French antiques and curiosities. Directly imported.

Ohmega Salvage
2407 San Pablo Avenue
Berkeley, CA 94702
510.843.7368
Architectural elements, wrought iron, plaster flourishes, knobs, hinges, tubs, mantels, lighting, more.

Prize
2363 San Pablo Avenue
Berkeley, CA 94702
510.848.1168
Light, bright painted antique furniture with chintz-floral accents.

Treillage
418 East 75th Street
New York, NY 10021
212.535.2288
also in the Gump's store,
135 Post Street
San Francisco, CA 94108
415.982.1616
The finest of garden ornament and furniture.

Yardart
2188½ Sutter Street
San Francisco, CA 94115
415.346.6002
Antique and near antique garden ornament, of small and large scale.

Zonal
568 Hayes Street
San Francisco, CA 94102
415.255.9307
Postwar porch and garden furniture, as well as indoor iron beds, hutches, etc.

Home Accessories

Botanica
1633 West Lewis Street
San Diego, CA 92103
619.294.3100
Stylish floral design, smart, chic accessories.

The Gardener
1836 Fourth Street
Berkeley, CA 94710
510.548.4545
Fine merchandise inspired by the garden, from rugs to vases, all of impeccable design.

Garden Home
1799 Fourth Street
Berkeley, CA 94710
510.559.7050
Interior furniture, topiary, orchids, accessories inspired by the garden.

George
2411 California Street
San Francisco, CA 94115
415.441.0564
Cat grass, and the neatest accessories for the animals of your garden home.

Le Jardin du Soleil
415.331.1114
Exquisite reproduction French wrought iron garden furniture. Handmade by special order.

Maison d'Etre
5330 College Avenue
Oakland, CA 94618
510.658.0698
Inspired gilded interior artifacts, many with a floral theme.

Paxton Gate
1204 Stevenson Street
San Francisco, CA 94103
415.255.5955
The oddest garden store of all. Taxidermy mice, butterflies, bugs, fine Japanese tools, bromeliad topiaries.

Pier One Imports
Stores nationwide.
800.245.4595
Mosquito netting, candles, etc.

Restoration Hardware
Stores nationwide and catalog.
800.762.1005
Witty and well-resourced home products and furniture.

RH
2506 Sacramento Street
San Francisco, CA 94115
415.346.1460
Herb topiaries, terrace furniture, dinnerware.

Smith & Hawken
Stores nationwide and catalog.
800.776.3336
Garden accessories, furniture, books, etc.

Sue Fisher King
3067 Sacramento Street
San Francisco, CA 94115
415.922.7276
Linens, bath, and tableware of the
highest quality.

Nurseries & Suppliers

Cedros Gardens
330 S. Cedros Avenue
Solana Beach, CA 92075
619.792.8640
Plants with a slant toward natives, but
with all the fun of the wild garden.
Rustic outdoor furniture.

Chelsea Garden Center
205 West 9th Avenue
New York, NY 10011
212.929.2477
Indoor and outdoor evergreens, trees,
containers.

Floorcraft Garden Center
550 Bayshore Boulevard
San Francisco, CA 94124
415.824.1900
Herbs, shade-loving plants,
citrus, etc.

Four Winds Wholesale Nursery
42186 Palm Avenue
Fremont, CA 94539

Box 3538
Mission San Jose District
Fremont, CA 94539
510.656.2591
Citrus specimens, small to large, pink
lemons to kaffir limes and Buddha's
hands. Very complete.

Hortica
566 Castro Street
San Francisco, CA 94114
415.863.4697
Indoor plants, water gardens, orchids,
containers, hothouse grown plants, etc.

Potted Gardens
27 Bedford Street
New York, NY 10014
212.255.4797
Container gardening with
a sassy, resourceful angle.

Sloat Garden Center
San Francisco Bay Area locations,
415.566.4415
Plants for the indoor and outdoor
garden, containers.

Invaluable Resources

The Apple Farm
18501 Greenwood Road
Philo, CA 95466
707.895.2333
The Bates and the Schmitts—artists of
food, apple farming, rammed earth
building design, flower gardening, and
purveyors of delicious chutneys, jams
juices, and more. Renowned cooking
school here too, run by Sally Schmitt.

The Boonville Hotel
14050 Hwy. 128
Boonville, CA 95415

Box 326
Boonville, CA 95415
707.895.2210
John Schmitt's stylish hotel in the
Anderson Valley, near Mendocino, has
the feel of a garden house, including a
new building where one really reaps
the benefits of indoor-outdoor living.
Excellent cuisine and a palate-quenching
wine selection, too.

Cliff's Hardware and Home
479 Castro Street
San Francisco, CA 94114
415.431.5365
Like an old five-and-dime, with everything one would need to fulfill creative
endeavors.

Jeffrey Doney
2200 Pacific Avenue #6E
San Francisco, CA 94115
415.567.1967
Landscape and interior design.

Rayon Vert
3187 Sixteenth Street
San Francisco, CA 94103
415.861.3516
Kelly Kornigay's creations with flowers
and branches are a wonder. Vases,
lighting, furniture, and accessories, too.

Your Space
161 Natoma Street
San Francisco, CA 94105
415.357.9800
Interior design, planning.